FIRST CHAPT

TIME
CHRONICLE
READ WITH
Biff,
Chip &
Kipper

The Jewel in the Hub

Written by David Hunt
and illustrated by Alex Brychta

OXFORD
UNIVERSITY PRESS

Before reading

- Read the back cover text and page 4. What dangers do you think there could be for the children on their mission?
- Look at page 5. In what way do you think the Hub is like a computer hard drive?

After reading

- What do we find out about Leonardo from the story? Use books and the internet to find out more about Leonardo's life and inventions.

Book quiz

1 What did Leonardo and Wilf have to find in the cathedral?
   a The Hub
   b A parachute
   c The Blue Eye
2 Who appears in the doorway of the cathedral?
3 How does Leo stop the Hub from being stolen?

See p45 for the book quiz answers!

The story so far ...

Virans are a virus spreading through time. Their purpose is to bring about chaos and darkness.

Mortlock, the Time Guardian, has one last hope of defeating the Virans – the TimeWeb. Can the children go back in time, recover parts of the TimeWeb and return safely? Or will the mission be too difficult and dangerous?

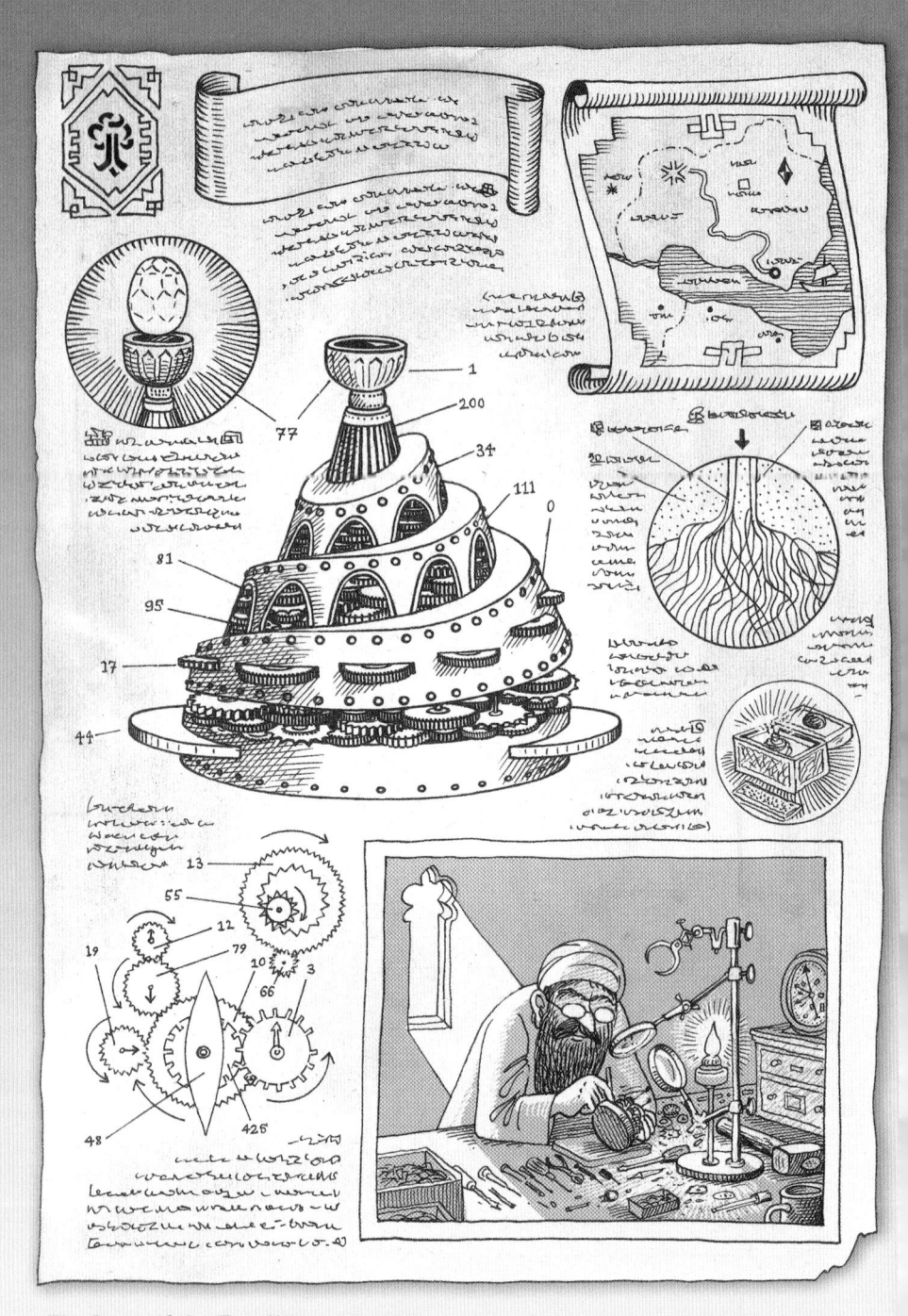

The Parts of the TimeWeb – the Hub

"... the Hub is a bit like the hard drive of a computer ..."

Theodore Mortlock – Time Guardian

Chapter 1

The Circularium sent Wilf spinning back in time. He felt as if he was falling forever, yet within seconds it had stopped. He had arrived.

He had no idea where the time machine had taken him. All he knew was that he was by himself. And in front of him was a half-open doorway.

Wilf gently pushed the door, and stepped through.

The room was icy cold. In front of him was a darkness as thick as smoke. From the darkness came muffled voices and the sounds of banging and crashing.

Wilf's heart pounded. The icy cold and darkness meant only one thing. Virans!

"It's not here," a voice rasped.

Then there were footsteps ... coming towards him!

To the side of him, Wilf could make out a low bench. He ducked down and wriggled under it.

"I wish the others were with me," he shuddered.

The footsteps came closer. Wilf held his breath, trying to make himself as small as he could. Then a shiver ran down his spine. A hand gripped his arm!

A voice whispered, "Ssh!" The voice was so close that Wilf could feel warm breath. Someone else was hiding too.

Chapter 2

The footsteps passed by. The door was slammed so hard that it shook the floor. The steps died away. Then silence.

The darkness slowly drained away. Wilf slid out from under the bench. A boy crawled out after him.

"Who are you?" the boy asked.

"Mortlock sent me," stuttered Wilf.

"Ah, Mortlock!" gasped the boy. "The Time Guardian! I've been expecting you. So those men must have been Virans."

Wilf saw he was in a workshop. But it was in a terrible mess. Tools, brushes, books, as well as half-finished statues and paintings, had been thrown to the floor. The boy began to look for something.

"We need to be careful," he said. "The Virans may come back."

"Where, exactly, am I?" asked Wilf.

"In Florence," the boy said. "It is 1468. My name is Leo and I am training to be an artist. I am learning many skills. At the moment I am studying architecture."

"Architecture? You mean buildings and stuff?" asked Wilf.

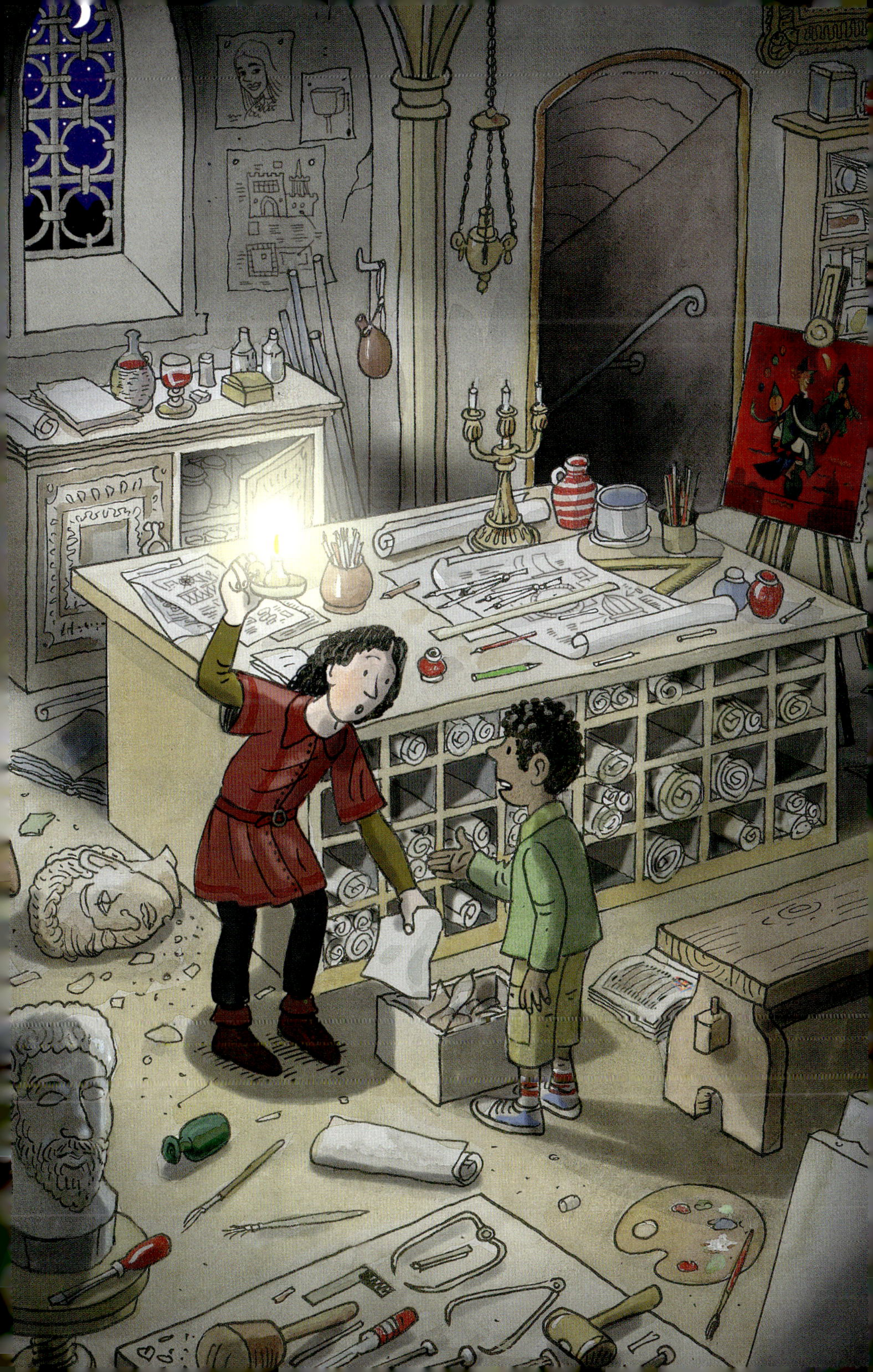

Leo nodded. "I am helping to complete the work on the new cathedral," he said.

He picked up the head of a smashed statue and looked at it sadly. "This is a statue of the architect who started work on the cathedral. He made this statue of himself to go inside it when it is finished."

"He must be a great man," said Wilf. "Is this his studio?"

"Yes," said Leo. "But he's gone. As well as being an architect, he was also a Time Guardian, like Mortlock. He left something for me to give to you. It's what the Virans were looking for."

Leo looked at the books on the floor. "Ah!" He seized an enormous book and flipped it open. "Thank goodness!" he breathed. "They didn't find it."

The middle of the book had been cut out. Hidden inside was a machine made of hundreds of gold cogs and springs. It was so beautiful that it made Wilf gasp.

It was the Hub.

Leo carefully took the machine out of the book.

"I've never seen anything like it before," he said. "But it doesn't work."

Wilf's heart sank. "That's because something's missing." He pointed to a hole in the centre of the machine. "I know what it is," he said. "Mortlock showed me a diagram of it. There should be a jewel in the centre."

Wilf wondered if the architect had hidden the jewel somewhere. He looked at the broken head of the statue.

It was then he noticed a crack across the left eye. "Look, Leo!" he gasped.

In the crack was a tiny scroll of paper. He pulled the paper out and unrolled it.

On the scroll was written:

*Where the Sun first looks on ground,
There the Blue Eye can be found.*

"I think I've seen the Blue Eye before," said Wilf. "It's the jewel! But how are we going to find it? I'm no good at solving riddles like this."

Leo laughed. "I am! I think I know where the Blue Eye can be found." He carefully wrapped the Hub in a silk bag. "Come on!"

Chapter 3

The dark, cobbled streets were eerily quiet. Wilf shivered. It was bitterly cold.

"I've never known it so cold," said Leo. "Maybe it will warm up as the sun rises."

"Where are we going?" asked Wilf.

"To the cathedral, where the Blue Eye is hidden. We must be inside before sunrise."

They pushed on in silence. They did not notice the two black shadows following them down the narrow streets.

At last they reached the city square. In front of them was an enormous domed building. Even though it was partly covered in wooden scaffolding, it was a magnificent sight.

Leo took a ring of keys from his belt and unlocked a small side door.

Chapter 4

Inside the cathedral, they looked up at the massive dome high above them. Leo's voice echoed around the space. *"Where the Sun first looks on ground, There the Blue Eye can be found."*

"When the sun rises," said Leo, "its beams will shine through one of the windows at the top and down to the floor."

"I get it!" said Wilf. "Whatever part of the floor the sunlight hits first is where the Blue Eye is hidden."

"Exactly," said Leo.

Within a moment, the top of the dome began to glow.

"Any moment now," whispered Leo.

A bright shaft of sunlight shone through a window, down to the floor.

"There!" shouted Wilf. They ran to the spot and pulled up the marble slab.

To their surprise it came away easily. Beneath the slab was a bundle of cloth.

"This must be it," said Wilf.

Wrapped in the cloth was a blue sapphire the size of a large marble.

"It's the Blue Eye!" said Wilf.

The crystal gleamed in the shaft of sunlight. Leo placed it into the Hub. It fitted perfectly. "Now it should work," he said.

The tiny cogs in the Hub began to turn. The Blue Eye burned with light, but only for a second. In the vast space above them was a huge web of shimmering light. Then it was gone.

"It's part of a bigger machine – the TimeWeb," said Wilf. "It won't work properly until it's all put together."

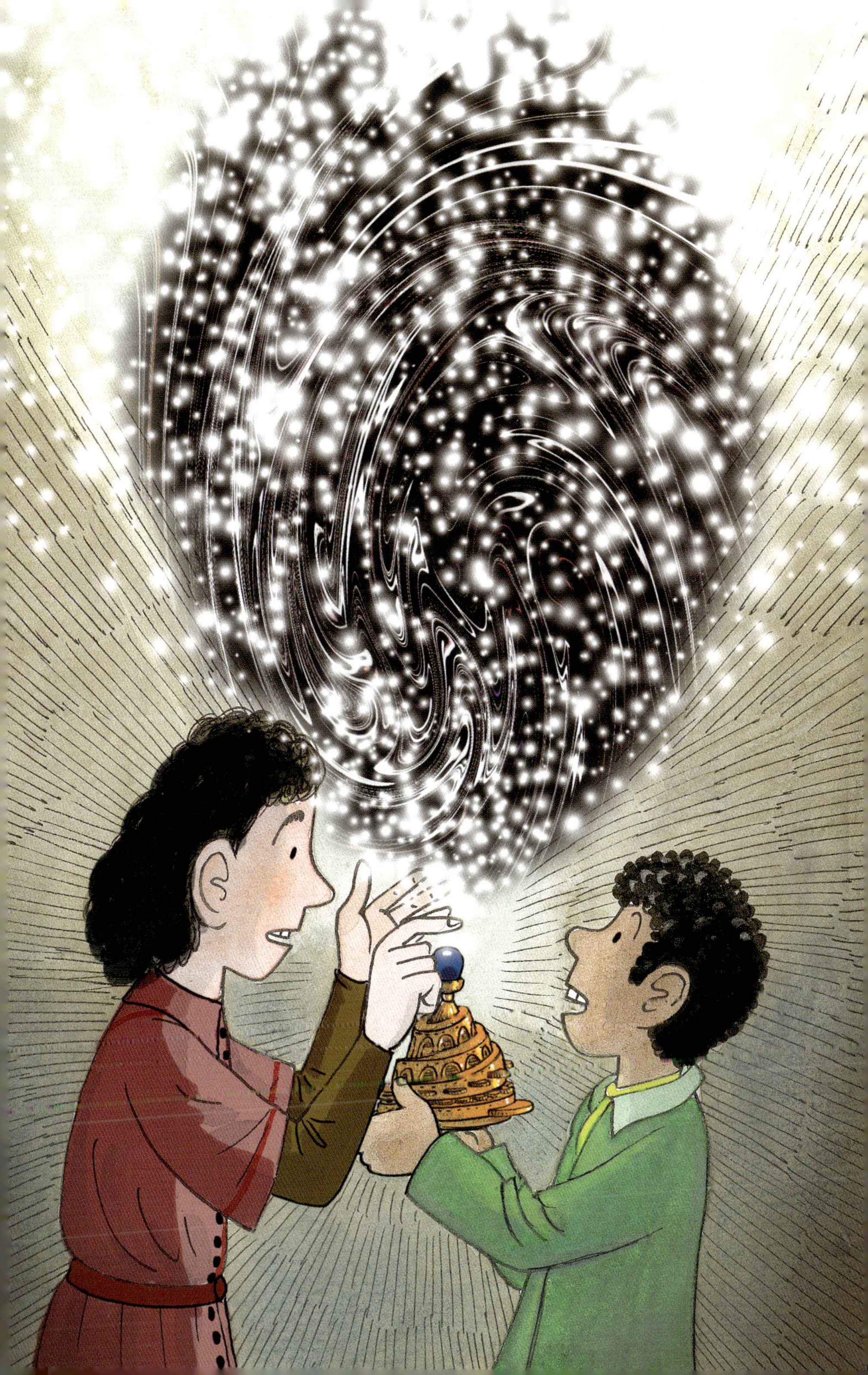

Then the daylight faded. In the doorway were two shadowy figures. They oozed darkness. It swirled around them like black ink dropped in water.

"Virans!" shouted Leo. "Run!"

There was only one way to go. They took the narrow stairs that led up to the top of the dome.

Chapter 5

Because the stairs twisted steeply, they could not see the Virans behind them. But they could hear them – a strange rasping sound that grew louder with every step.

Suddenly, Leo turned sharply and burst through a hatch into bright sunlight. Wilf followed, dazed, breathless and dizzy.

They were on the wooden scaffold high up outside the dome. At one end was a platform leading out to a large crane. Wilf's stomach turned as he looked over the edge.

The Virans had got to the hatch. They calmly walked towards them. Wilf was scared. They were trapped.

"What now?" he shouted.

A Viran gestured to the Hub. Leo was fumbling with it.

"Give!" hissed the Viran, holding out his hands.

"Leo! We have no choice," said Wilf.

The Viran stepped forward. Leo stared into his pale, cold eyes.

"Never!" he said, and he threw the Hub as far as he could over the edge of the scaffolding.

Wilf watched as it fell. "No!" he shouted.

Chapter 6

Suddenly, a tiny parachute opened, and the Hub floated safely to the ground.

"A little invention of mine," Leo smiled. He had tied the silk bag to the side of the Hub before he threw it and it had opened up like a parachute.

The Virans scrambled through the hatch. They had started the long climb down to get the Hub.

Wilf ran to the hatch. "Quick!" he said.

"Wait!" said Leo. "We'll never beat them on the stairs."

"Then we've failed!" said Wilf.

Leo went to the end of the platform. He was holding out a rope. "We'll take the crane!" he said. "Climb on to the cradle and hold tight."

He untied the cradle, and they swung out into mid-air. They dropped quickly. Wilf couldn't look. He closed his eyes and hung on tight.

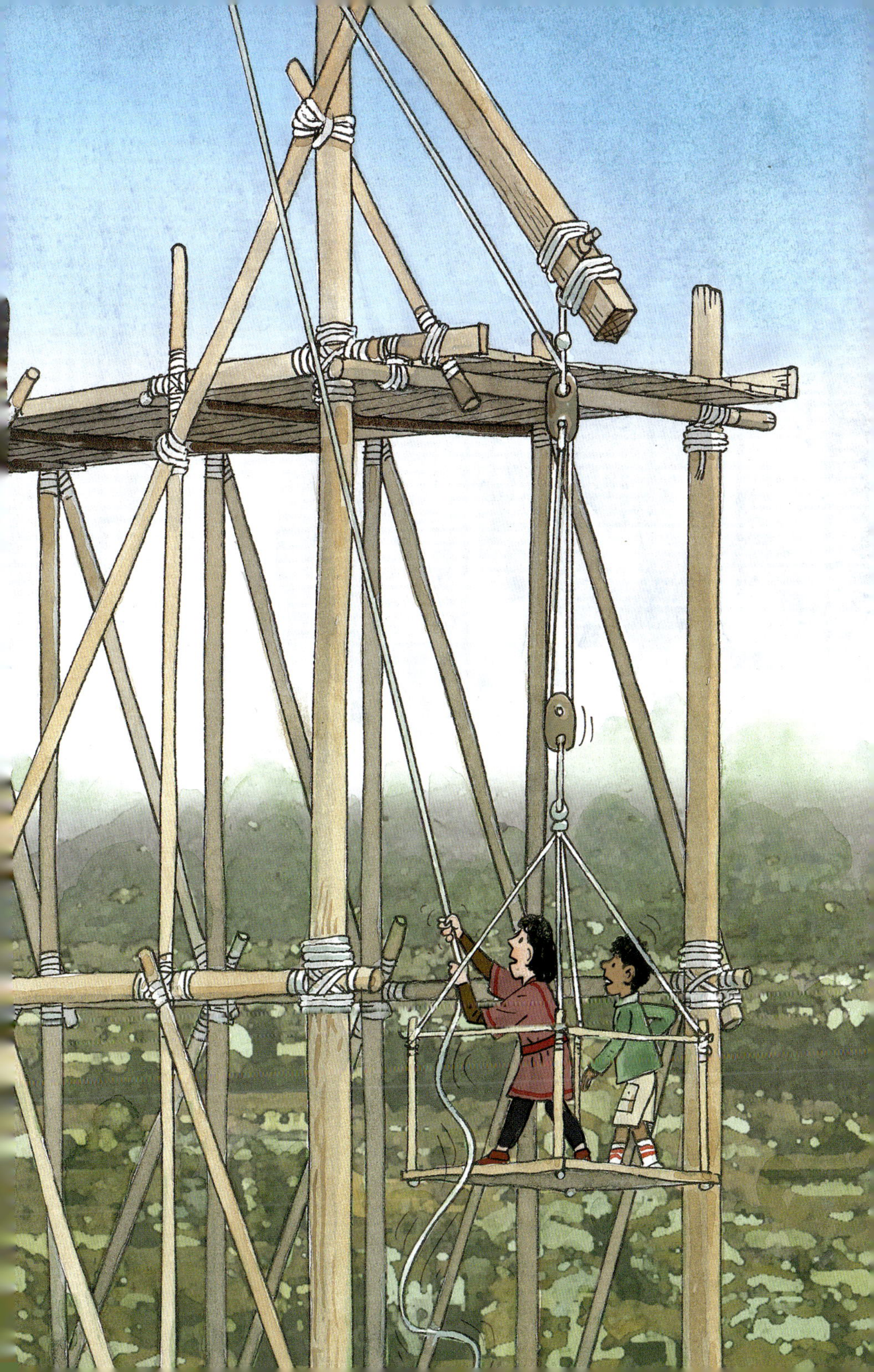

As they crashed to the ground, Wilf jumped from the cradle and picked up the Hub. Leo ran and locked the cathedral door. "Let's go. They'll be trapped inside for a few hours at least."

As they ran back through the streets of the city, Wilf saw a door that he *knew* was the way back to the Time Vault.

He held the Hub firmly, stood in the doorway and raised his hand in salute to Leo.

"That was brilliant," he said. "I'll never forget you. You were something else."

Leo smiled. "Me?" he said. "Something else? Not really, I'm just plain Leonardo from a little town in Italy called Vinci."

But Wilf had vanished.

Now what?

The box is safe. Wilf has found the Hub. But could Wilf have done it without Leo?

And who was the boy Leo from the small village of Vinci, and how did he know so much?

The Virans got close this time. They only have to find one piece of the TimeWeb and Mortlock will be finished. Will the children be able to outwit them every time?

Find out by reading the following:

The Matrix Mission or

The Power of the Cell

... Every second is precious, so hurry!

History: downloaded!
Leonardo da Vinci

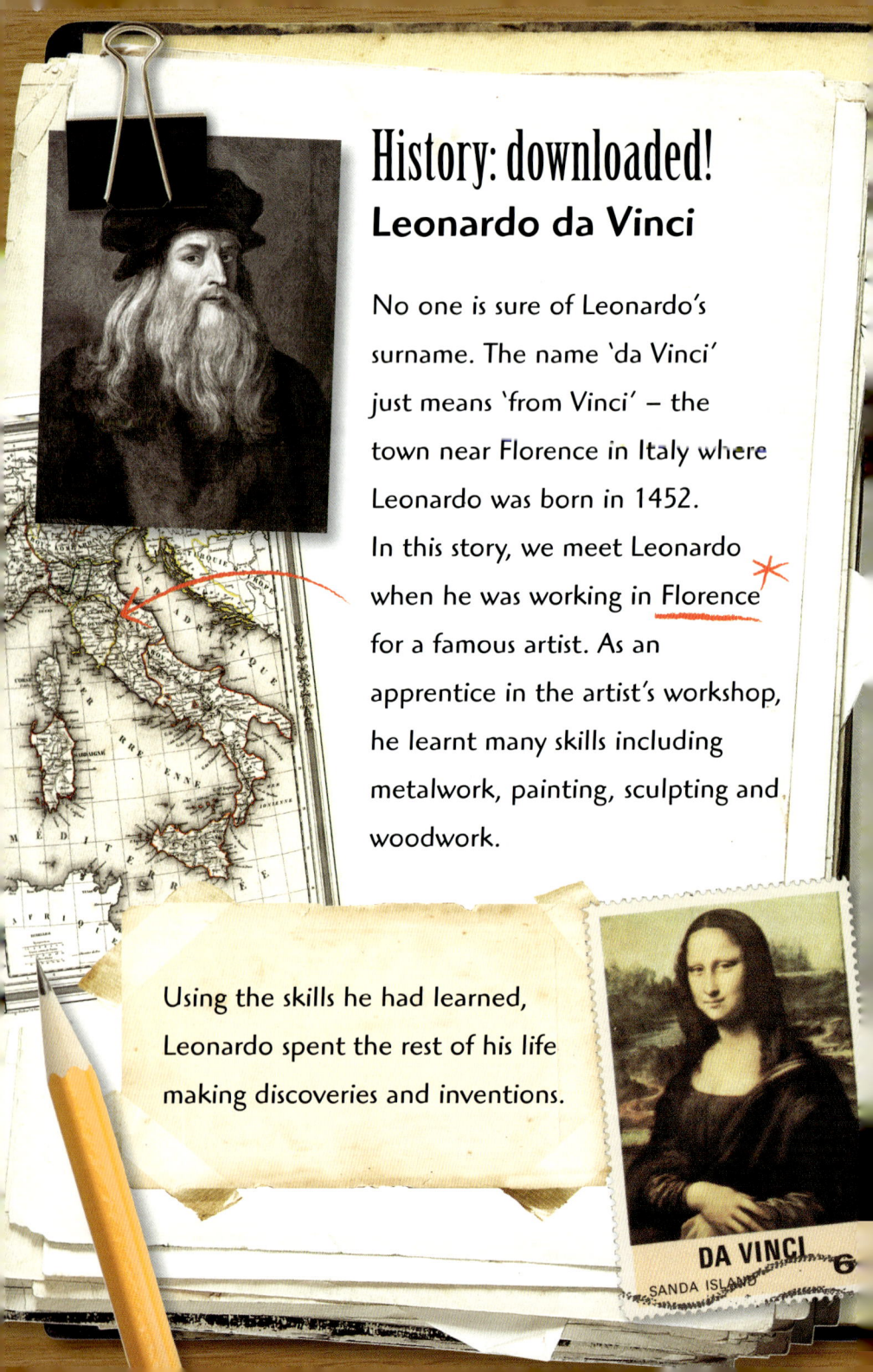

No one is sure of Leonardo's surname. The name 'da Vinci' just means 'from Vinci' – the town near Florence in Italy where Leonardo was born in 1452. In this story, we meet Leonardo when he was working in Florence for a famous artist. As an apprentice in the artist's workshop, he learnt many skills including metalwork, painting, sculpting and woodwork.

Using the skills he had learned, Leonardo spent the rest of his life making discoveries and inventions.

DA VINCI
SANDA ISLAND

In Leonardo's time, there were not many books, and so Leonardo got most of his ideas from studying nature. He made some great discoveries and invented many things that we can still learn from today.

or example, Leonardo drew plans for a crane

and a parachute

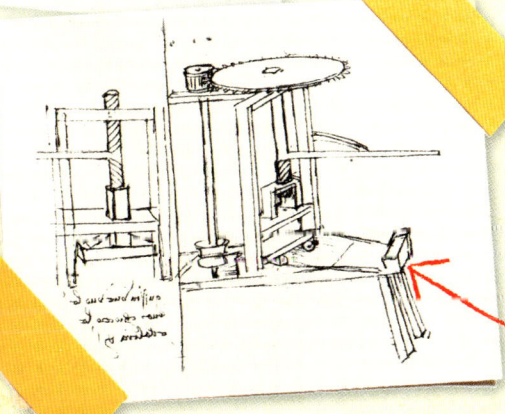

and worked on improving the printing press.

For more information, see the Time Chronicles website:
www.oxfordprimary.co.uk/timechronicles

Glossary

cathedral *(page 13)* The most important Christian church in an area. The main priest of a cathedral is usually a bishop or archbishop. *"I am helping to complete the work on the new cathedral,"* he said.

cobbled *(page 20)* A road made of small, rounded stones known as 'cobbles'. An old type of road or pavement. *The dark, cobbled streets were eerily quiet.*

cradle *(page 33)* A platform that is suspended by ropes. Used to carry people, tools or stone up the side of a building. *He untied the cradle, and they swung out into mid-air.*

dazed *(page 28)* Unable to think clearly. Many things can daze you, from a bang to the head, to simply being amazed by something! *Wilf followed, dazed, breathless and dizzy.*

muffled *(page 7)* A sound that is not clear. It is as if the sound has had to come through something, like a wall for example. *From the darkness came muffled voices ...*

rasped *(page 8)* A rough, scraping, grating sound. The word 'rasp' sounds like the noise itself. *"It's not here,"* a voice rasped.

Have you read them all yet?

Level 11:

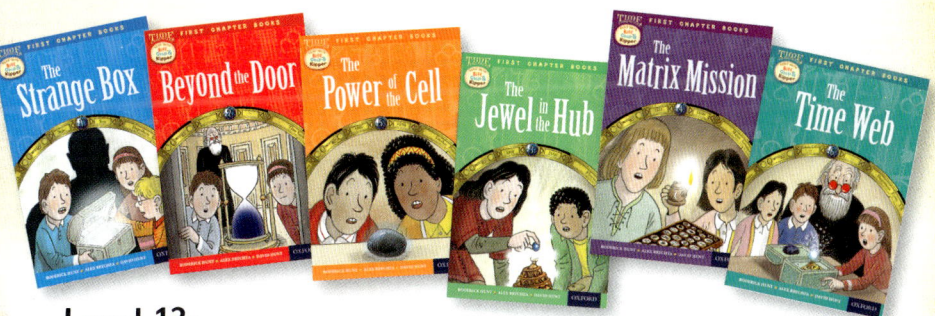

The Strange Box • Beyond the Door • The Power of the Cell • The Jewel in the Hub • The Matrix Mission • The Time Web

Level 12:

Time Runners

Tyler: His Story

A Jack and Three Queens

Mission Victory

The Enigma Plot

The Thief Who Stole Nothing

More great fiction from Oxford Children's:

www.winnie-the-witch.com

www.dinosaurcove.co.uk

About the Authors

Roderick Hunt MBE - creator of best-loved characters Biff, Chip, Kipper, Floppy and their friends. His first published stories were those he told his two sons at bedtime. Rod lives in Oxfordshire, in a house not unlike the house in the Magic Key adventures. In 2008, Roderick received an MBE for services to education, particularly literacy.

Roderick Hunt's son **David Hunt** was brought up on his father's stories and knows the world of Biff, Chip and Kipper intimately. His love of history and a good story has sparked many new ideas, resulting in the *Time Chronicles* series. David has had a successful career in the theatre, most recently working on scripts for Jude Law's *Hamlet* and *Henry V*, as well as Derek Jacobi's *Twelfth Night*.

Joint creator of the best-loved characters Biff, Chip, Kipper, Floppy and their friends, **Alex Brychta MBE** has brought each one to life with his fabulous illustrations, which are known and loved in many schools today. Following the Russian occupation of Czechoslovakia, Alex Brychta moved with his family from Prague to London. He studied graphic design and animation, before moving to the USA where he worked on animation for Sesame Street. Since then he has devoted many years of his career to *Oxford Reading Tree*, bringing detail, magic and humour to every story! In 2012 Alex received an MBE for services to children's literature.

Roderick Hunt and Alex Brychta won the prestigious Outstanding Achievement Award at the Education Resources Awards in 2009.

Levelling info for parents

What do the levels mean?

Read with Biff Chip & Kipper First Chapter Books have been designed by educational experts to help children develop as readers.

Each book is carefully levelled to allow children to make gradual progress and to feel confident and enjoy reading.

The Oxford Levels you will see on these books are used by teachers and are based on years of research in schools. Below is a summary of what each Oxford Level means, so that you can help your child to improve and enjoy their reading.

The books at Level 11 (Brown Book Band):

At this level, the sentence structures are becoming longer and more complex. The story plot may be more involved and there is a wider vocabulary. However, the proportion of unknown words used per paragraph/page is still carefully controlled to help build their reading stamina and allow children to read independently.

This level mostly covers characterisation through characters' actions and words rather than through description. The story may be organised in various ways, e.g. chronologically, thematically, sequentially, as relevant to the text type and subject.

The books at Level 12 (Grey Book Band):

At this level, the sentences are becoming more varied in structure and length. Though still straightforward, more inference may be required, e.g. in dialogue to work out who is speaking. Again, the story may be organised in various ways: chronologically, thematically, sequentially, etc., so that children can reflect on how the organisation helps the reader to understand the text.

The *Times Chronicles* books are also ideal for older children who feel less confident and need more practice in order to build stamina. The text is written to be age and ability appropriate, but also engaging, motivating and funny, making them a pleasure for children to read at this stage of their reading development.

OXFORD
UNIVERSITY PRESS

Great Clarendon Street, Oxford, OX2 6DP,
United Kingdom

Oxford University Press is a department of the University of Oxford.
It furthers the University's objective of excellence in research, scholarship,
and education by publishing worldwide. Oxford is a registered trade mark
of Oxford University Press in the UK and in certain other countries

Text © Roderick Hunt and David Hunt

Text written by David Hunt, based on the original characters
created by Roderick Hunt and Alex Brychta

Illustrations © Alex Brychta

The moral rights of the authors have been asserted

Database rights Oxford University Press (maker)

First published 2010
This edition published in 2014

All rights reserved. No part of this publication may be reproduced, stored
ina retrieval system, or transmitted, in any form or by any means, without
the prior permission in writing of Oxford University Press, or as expressly
permitted by law, by licence or under terms agreed with the appropriate
reprographics rights organization. Enquiries concerning reproduction
outside the scope of the above should be sent to the Rights Department,
Oxford University Press, at the address above.

You must not circulate this work in any other form
and you must impose this same condition on any acquirer

British Library Cataloguing in Publication Data
Data available

978-0-19-273907-0

1 3 5 7 9 10 8 6 4 2

Paper used in the production of this book is a natural, recyclable product
made from wood grown in sustainable forests. The manufacturing process
conforms to the environmental regulations of the country of origin.

Printed in China

Acknowledgements: The publisher and authors would like to thank the following
for their permission to reproduce photographs and other copyright material:

P38tr TsR/Shutterstock; **P38tl** INTERFOTO/Alamy; **P38ml** Steven Wright/
Shutterstock; **P38bl** Valeriy Aksak/Shutterstock; **P38m** Valentin Agapov/
Shutterstock; **P38br** Ken Brown/Shutterstock; **P38-39** Jakub Krechowicz/
Shutterstock; Blaz Kure/Shutterstock; **P39ml** SSPL/Getty Images; **P39mr**
SSPL/Getty Images; **P39bl** SSPL/Getty Images.

Book quiz answers
1 c
2 Two Virans
3 He sends it to the ground in a parachute, then locks the Virans inside the cathedral.